W9-DIT-932

THE COMPLETE GUIDE TO CHIP CARVING

WAYNE BARTON

Sterling Publishing Co., Inc.
New York

To Marlies, for your loving devotion to our family

Library of Congress Cataloging-in-Publication Data

Barton, Wayne.

  The complete guide to chip carving / Wayne Barton.

    p. cm.

  Includes index.

  ISBN-13: 978-1-4027-4128-9

  ISBN-10: 1-4027-4128-6

  1. Wood-carving. 2. Wood-carving—Patterns. I. Title.

TT199.7.B372 2007

736'.4—dc22

                            2006024108

10 9 8 7 6 5 4 3 2 1

Published by Sterling Publishing Co., Inc.

387 Park Avenue South, New York, NY 10016

© 2007 by Wayne Barton

Distributed in Canada by Sterling Publishing

c/o Canadian Manda Group, 165 Dufferin Street

Toronto, Ontario, Canada M6K 3H6

Distributed in the United Kingdom by GMC Distribution Services,

Castle Place, 166 High Street, Lewes, East Sussex, England BN7 1XU

Distributed in Australia by Capricorn Link (Australia) Pty. Ltd.

P.O. Box 704, Windsor, NSW 2756, Australia

Sterling ISBN-13: 978-1-4027-4128-9

  ISBN-10: 1-4027-4128-6

For information about custom editions, special sales, premium

and corporate purchases, please contact Sterling Special Sales

Department at 800-805-5489 or specialsales@sterlingpub.com.

CONTENTS

PREFACE

IN THE FOLLOWING PAGES, you will embark on a carving journey that will be a source of immense satisfaction for the rest of your life. The instruction presented here is unquestionably the finest guidance ever available for the aspiring chip carver. It is the product of one man's lifetime of study in the art, and decades of teaching countless people like you the proper methods used in this unique form of carving.

Wayne Barton is the most renowned chip carver in the world. Many others have attempted their own teaching of this particular endeavor via books, personal instruction, and DVDs. With few exceptions, most instructors in the United States and Canada who are now passing on the knowledge of chip-carving methods, were introduced to the art by exposure to Wayne and/or his classes and writings. However, it remains true today that none have reached the level of Wayne in either range or depth of execution techniques and artistic design, nor equaled his remarkable ability to describe and instruct others in chip carving.

On a limited scale, chip carving was present on this side of the Atlantic Ocean for years but has proliferated in North America only over the past quarter century. Single-handedly, Wayne Barton has been the driving force behind the recognition and renaissance that chip carving has enjoyed both here and abroad. This large-scale introduction of chip carving and the magnificent levels attainable by executing this style of carving began when Wayne published his first article on the subject in 1984. However, Wayne had been committed to this type of carving for many years prior to that article. The woodcarving population at large became acquainted with the style as a result of his regular column in *Chip Chats*, the magazine of the National Wood Carvers Association, his books and videotape, numerous appearances on television, and his classes. Owing to his inspired example, chip carving is today commonplace in almost all woodcarving shows, to the point of comprising a distinct category in most competitions.

As a young man, Wayne Barton made a decision to pursue a life in carving. Rather than take a "learn-as-you-go" approach, he went to Brienz, Switzerland, for formal study in all forms of the woodcarver's art under the tutelage of some of the masters still actively carving and teaching there. Upon his return to the States, he taught at the Chicago School of Woodcarving before establishing the Alpine School of Woodcarving, Ltd., focusing on chip carving as a specialty. Throughout the course of his career, he didn't pay great attention to gaining personal accolades. Although he was awarded first place in every competition he entered, his focus has always been on teaching and sharing his knowledge with others. He has also been recognized by the Swiss National Museum in Zurich, which honored him by placing his work on special exhibition for 18 months. Wayne has appeared on public and educational TV on The *American Woodshop* with Scott Phillips and The *Woodwright's Shop* with Roy Underhill.

Long before anyone else, Wayne recognized the need for superior carving tools. As a result, he developed the Wayne Barton Premier Chip Carving Knives, which are now in common use worldwide and recognized as the best available for their superior quality and ergonomic design. He has also developed easy-to-use ceramic sharpening stones that are unsurpassed. With no more than two knives and his extraordinary skills, Wayne Barton introduced us to this art form. He continues to create his magnificent carvings which are enjoyed and copied by so many others today.

I am fortunate to be one of the many carvers who are happily engaged in the practice of chip carving. In many cases, this was made possible entirely through Wayne Barton's writing on this carving specialty. The pages that follow present the sixth book Wayne has written on the subject. It is the culmination and distillation of almost 50 years of his personal chip-carving knowledge in one reference work, all the skills required for any chip carving—from the simplest to the most complex. Having been exposed to the entire spectrum of chip-carving information available over the past twenty-some years, I can attest to the fact that the following pages cannot be equaled for jump-starting your knowledge and skills. Read, absorb, practice, and enjoy!

—David W. Crothers
Hatboro, PA

Acknowledgments

I HAVE HAD SUCH GOOD FORTUNE throughout my carving career to be blessed with an extraordinary number of friends in the carving world, rare in talent, warm in friendship, and charitable in spirit. Their collective encouragement can be found on every page of this book. Not wanting to risk the omission of any, I would like to say at once to all, thank you for what you've given and what we have shared—you know who you are.

Any acknowledgment would be incomplete without specifically mentioning the more than thirty years of invaluable collaboration, joyfully shared with Gottlieb Brandli, the finest of cabinetmakers and dearest of friends. His sense of humor and abundant knowledge are only part of what has made his friendship a treasure I cherish.

In terms of production, I am indebted to Colleen Barker, who most professionally and artfully produced all the photography herein. Her skills are wrapped in personal charm. In addition, my appreciation goes to my son-in-law, Michael Auriemma, who patiently and willingly lent his hands for the carving photographs, for he is right-handed and I am not. Many thanks to my dear friend and secretary, Joanne Inda, who has faithfully kept the office running smoothly for more years than she'll tell, and gleefully corrects more than my spelling. Also, a very special thanks to my daughter, Heidi, for cheerfully lending her always-on-call typing skills, and expertise of how the English language is properly structured. As her father, it's humbling.

Acknowledgment must be given to my editor, Rodman Pilgrim Neumann, for his superb effort and accomplishment in arranging the material submitted to him for this book. His suggestions, patience, and editorial skills have rendered this work more easily understood.

Most of all, words inadequately express my love and gratitude to my wife, Marlies, who, with encouragement, humor, moral support, and abundant love, has buoyantly seen this project through. Thanks again, Marlies, as always.

CHIP CARVING

WOODCARVING AS A NOUN speaks of an extraordinary tactile art form. As a verb, woodcarving is the adventure of rendering that art form in any number of carving disciplines and styles. Chip carving is one of those disciplines, deriving its name from the way wood is removed in the process of carving.

Most carving disciplines require the carver to remove wood by shaving, as when whittling with a knife or sculpting with chisels and gouges. When power equipment is employed, the wood is ground away.

Chip carving is a decorative style of carving. Rather than sculpting or shaping wood, chip carving is applied to an object or piece that is already finished or shaped. It is executed by making very precise, angled cuts that enable the wood to be removed in the form of geometric chips of a specific size, shape, and proportion. Design aside, properly executed, attractive chip carving is distinguished by chips with smooth single facets, clean grooves, and sharp ridges.

The essence of chip carving is simplicity and versatility. It is a decorative style of carving that is quickly and easily learned when practiced. It is simple in tool use and execution, versatile in design possibilities and application.

Because of its simplicity, chip carving may be able to claim the title of oldest style of woodcarving. Our ancestors making rudimentary designs by carving notches and grooves in stone is a prehistoric fact—which may also indicate that man has an innate predisposition to express himself artistically. It is reasonable to assume that similar activity was practiced in a more readily available and softer material, namely wood, as it has been for centuries by indigenous cultures around the world.

Through time an exchange of motifs between countries has obscured the origin of certain designs. However, chip carving as it is enjoyed today in many English-speaking countries finds its roots in Europe and, particularly, Great Britain.

As an art form and delightful, functional pastime, chip carving in recent years has been experiencing a renaissance. This again may be attributed to the charm of its simplicity. Included also would be its broad, seemingly endless application for decorating objects from the simple, such as, plates, plaques, and boxes, to the more elaborate, such as, mantels, ceiling beams, and furniture. Also, the personal satisfaction derived from one's own creativity cannot be discounted, for art, in its many forms, is the soul of civilization. From this, one could correctly conclude that the pleasures of chip carving, with a little study and practice, are available to everyone.

For the purpose of design distinction or identification, various chip-carving motifs and patterns are sometimes described as belonging to a particular style. Any composition may incorporate one or several design styles. It first must be understood that all chip carving, of whatever design style, is produced by incising, i.e., making cuts into the wood to remove chips to create a design, whatever that may be called.

Negative patterns are made by removing chips, the total of which provides the desired design. That design is revealed by what is seen below the surface of the wood. Positive patterns are made by cutting away background chips, revealing the design at the surface of the wood. It is often possible to make both a negative and a positive carving from the same design.

The design components or motifs of chip carving, both geometric and nongeometric, such as rosettes, grids, freeform, and positive imaging, may be found singularly in a carving or in combination with others. The various borders, rosettes, and grids are combined and interchanged—creating entirely different designs, all primarily from variations of two- and - three cornered chips alone. Though unfamiliar to the novice, with practice, these design elements are not difficult to master.

All of these are described and illustrated herein along with lettering, tools used, how to sharpen a knife perfectly for a carving, which wood to use, finishing, and numerous hints to make your carving an easier and more enjoyable experience.

This book is a complete step-by-step guide for anyone wanting to learn the artful style of chip carving, a most decorative, functional, and creatively satisfying way to carve wood.

Easily studied, this book will encourage those who are inspired, fanning the artistic flame that burns within each one of us.

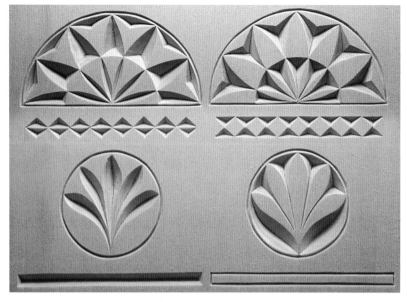

Negative.   **Positive.**

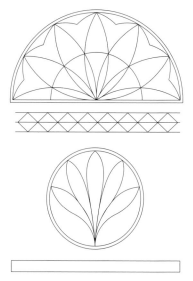

1

Tools and Materials

ONE OF THE UNEXPECTED pleasures of chip carving is discovering the limited number of tools and materials needed to do truly fine carving. And, unlike some other carving disciplines, acquiring additional tools will not increase your skill or produce a better finished product.

Knives

Ever since man has carved wood, the type of tools used has been dictated by the type of wood to be carved and the finished work desired. This is true for all styles and methods, including chip carving. When hard woods are used (meaning woods that are *physically hard*), skews, chisels, and a mallet serve best. Skews and chisels may also be used on softer woods with hand pressure alone, though design selection is limited by this method.

Today, chip carving is normally done in woods that are fairly easy to cut into with knives alone. This makes the process faster, easier, and more available to those who desire to carve for the pleasure of its simplicity, both in tools used and style employed. Knives used today, however, vary in number, quality, and configuration. Sets of knives labeled for chip carving may be found numbering from two to twenty-four, but only two will ever be needed to do all the carving shown within this book. After starting, it will soon be discovered that more is not necessary. When only two knives are used, give yourself every advantage. Cheap, inadequate tools produce only disappointing results, and are so often a waste of time and money.

The two WB Premier chip-carving knives used to execute all the carvings in this book were designed by the author. They are the result of a lifetime of carving and teaching, and are widely recognized as the finest available today, for several reasons. The blades are made of high-carbon true tool steel (not stainless) and are properly tempered to hold an edge longer.

The cutting knife (#1) is used to remove all wood and is the one most frequently employed. It has a short, broad blade for strength and workability. Its tip is more sharply pointed and downwardly angled, allowing the carver to make curved cuts more easily as well as execute tighter corners and niches. The stab knife (#2) gets it name from the way it is held. Rather than removing wood, it cuts and spreads the fibers, leaving a permanent, decorative wedge-shaped impression in the wood. It has a longer blade edge, allowing longer "stabs" to be made, increasing design possibilities. The stab knife may be said to complement the work of the cutting knife.

Although most work is done with the cutting knife, it is a mistake to disregard the importance and capabilities of the stab knife. Students who neglect the stab knife deny themselves the full possibilities of chip carving. Together, these two knives quickly and easily entice designs both simple and complex from the wood.

WB Premier Chip-Carving Knives #1 cutting (top), #2 stab (bottom).

Another significant advantage of these knives is their ergonomically designed handles. They have been shaped from domestic wood and offer an excellent grip for hours of comfortable, easy, non-fatiguing carving.

Sharpening Stones

Through the years, many materials have been used to sharpen carving tools, including a slurry of emery sand and goose grease, stones found in nature, diamond-crusted metal plates, and various interpretations of leather straps. All of them perform to a certain degree, some better than others. To a novice, choosing one is like a journey through a forest with many paths. To decide, it is best to know the destination.

There are three criteria for properly sharpened chip-carving knives. They are: a very sharp edge that is straight; an edge that is sharpened at the correct angle; and polishing the blade to a mirror finish. How to accomplish this is covered in Chapter 3, "How to Sharpen Chip Carving Knives." While many devices are available from which one may choose, ceramic sharpening stones have long been proven to be superbly effective in meeting these criteria. Their use is illustrated and recommended herein. However, if the reader has preferred alternative materials and/or methods for sharpening, that meet the necessary criteria, he/she is encouraged to continue with what is familiar and comfortable. As stated earlier, there are many paths through the forest.

Two ceramic stones should be sufficient, a medium-grade for shaping and sharpening, and an ultra fine for honing or polishing. It is important that both stones be absolutely flat to prevent rounding the tip or cupping the blade. A true ultrafine stone will highly polish a blade, eliminating the need for further preparation before carving.

Ceramic Sharpening Stones—medium (top) ultrafine (bottom).

Additional Materials

The remaining basic tools that are helpful to begin chip carving are: a small T-square (preferably one with both metric and imperial increments), a mechanical 0.05 pencil, and a drafting or bow-type compass. Using a grade B lead in both the compass and pencil will make legible lines without impressing or denting the wood. Being a softer grade of lead, B is much easier to erase than harder grades. Drawing light lines will make cleanup much easier, and using an ink eraser will do the job quickly and neatly.

FINDING THE TOOLS AND MATERIALS

The materials and tools shown and recommended in this book, including the boxes and basswood plates, are generally available from most woodcarving and woodworking suppliers. If there is difficulty locating them, contact the author for specific suppliers.

Wayne Barton
The Alpine School of Woodcarving
225 Vine Avenue
Park Ridge, IL 60068
847-692-2822 or fax 847-692-6626

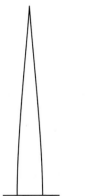

Correct angle to sharpen.

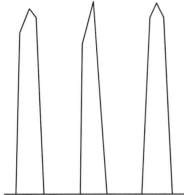

These three are incorrect.

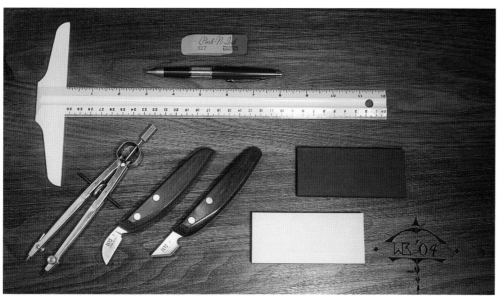

Tools needed for chip carving: mechanical 0.05 pencil, eraser, T-square ruler, draftsman's compass, WB Premier cutting and stab knives, and ceramic sharpening and polishing stones.

Woods for Chip Carving

WHILE NEARLY ALL WOODS have the potential of being carved, most of them for one or more reasons will not serve well for chip carving. Factors such as hardness, availability, having a wild grain or a highly figured grain will disqualify most.

Woods of greater density or hardness such as oak, maple, cherry and black walnut are best carved with the use of mallet and chisel, offering limited design potential for chip carving. Highly figured and exotic grained woods tend to obscure the efforts of the carver and are also generally too hard to be carved well with a knife. Some woods easily carved with a knife often have limited availability, may be difficult to acquire, and could prove to be more expensive than woods commonly chip carved. Jelutong (*Dyera costulata*) would be a good example.

Ideal Wood for Chip Carving

Chip carving described in this book is done exclusively with knives, as is most chip carving today. Like a painter expressing his art on a stretched canvas, wood is the canvas upon which a chip carver displays his work. The better the carver's canvas (or wood) performs, the better the carving. The ideal wood is one with a firm and tight straight grain, that is fairly common and inexpensive, and that is easily carved with a knife. This criterion is well met by basswood (*Tilia* spp.), which has been favored by carvers for centuries.

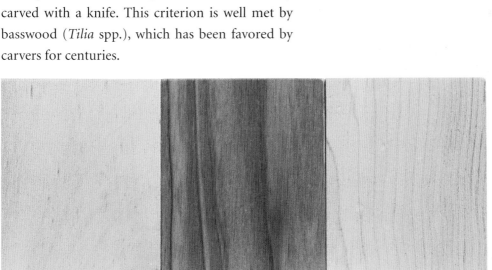

(Left to right) Basswood, butternut, white pine.

Classified as a hardwood, basswood is easy and satisfying to carve. It is pale cream to yellowish brown with a uniform fine texture. Basswood is essentially identical to what Europeans know as linden/lime. Linden is a family of trees—*Tiliaceae*—in which the genus Tilia is generally termed linden, and is native in temperate regions. The North American linden (*Tilia americana*) is commonly referred to as *basswood* or *whitewood*. This close-grained wood is most satisfying for any chip-carving project. Northern-grown basswood seems to perform better than southern because of its tighter grain.

Butternut (*Juglans cinera*) is also a hardwood. The heartwood is a light brown, frequently with pinkish tones or darker brown streaks. It is moderately light in weight (about the same as eastern white pine), rather coarse-textured, and moderately soft. It resembles black walnut and oak when stained. Like basswood, butternut is a joy to carve.

Eastern white pine (*Pinus strobus*) is sometimes confused with Ponderosa pine (*Pinus ponderosa*) and western white (*Pinus monticola*), and is also known in some areas as Weymouth pine, as well as by other names. This is a straight-grained, even-textured soft-wood that is good for chip carving, although it tends to split. Unlike some other pines, a knife cuts easily across the grain. The heartwood is light brown, often with a reddish tinge; exposure to air darkens the wood. Eastern white pine is inexpensive yet easy to work, and takes a polish well.

Among the woods that may be found locally but which are not broadly available, and will provide a level of satisfaction for chip carving, are catalpa (*Catalpa* spp.), tupelo (*Nyssa* spp.), buckeye (*Aesculus* spp.), cypress (*Cupressus sempervirens.*) or bald cypress (*Taxodium distichum*), black willow (*Salix nigra*), and Royal paulownia (*Paulownia tomentosa*).

Woods used for carving are almost never purchased at a traditional lumberyard or building supply store. They normally can be found at cabinet shops (which have the equipment to size lumber), hardwood lumberyards, woodworking and specialty wood stores, sawmills, and some craft stores.

Moisture Content

The one factor that most affects carving woods (indeed, all woods) is moisture content. Moisture content of eight to twelve percent, depending on the species, will hold wood fibers together nicely and lubricate the cutting tool. Wood that is too dry will audibly crunch and often crack away wood not intended to be removed.

Moisture can be added to wood in several ways, the best being slowly. Take a plastic bag large enough to accommodate the piece being carved and a pan of water. Place the pan of water in the bag. Then also place the piece in the bag in such a way that air can flow around it, and close the bag tight. Within one to three days the moisture content should be raised sufficiently to restore carving to a pleasant experience without crunching.

Moisture in an unfinished carving can be preserved by wrapping the carving in plastic or putting it in a plastic bag when not being worked on. Also, whenever possible, place the carving face down when the carving process is paused temporarily. This habit will not only help retain moisture on the carved surface, but because carving creates a greater drying area, this procedure will assist in keeping the wood from warping.

3

How to Sharpen Chip-Carving Knives

NOTHING WILL DISCOURAGE a potential carver faster than a knife that does not cut cleanly and smoothly. Conversely, nothing will give greater pleasure and satisfaction than one that does. To accomplish this in chip carving, cutting edges must be straight and ultrasharp, with the blade shaped correctly (particularly at the tip) and highly polished.

While there is no such thing as a one-and-only right way to sharpen a knife, a few suggestions will be helpful. It is not recommended that a power sharpener be used. Though such a device may produce a polished sharp edge, the use of a wheel and its speed is difficult to control when used on a knife that must keep a straight edge at a particular angle. It has a tendency to improperly shape the blade and round the tip, reducing its efficiency. Hand sharpening allows more control of the knife, which produces better results.

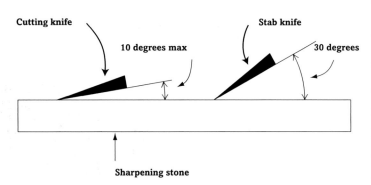

Angle for sharpening knives.

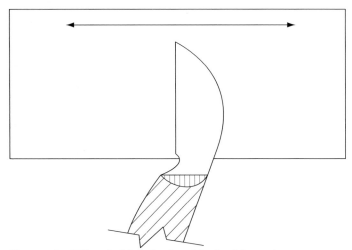

Sharpen by sliding the blade back and forth with equal pressure across the edge.

Sharpening by Hand

When sharpening by hand, there are two criteria that must be met: the stones used need to be both absolutely flat in order to keep the cutting edge straight, and wide enough to accommodate the entire cutting edge of the blade at once. Ceramic sharpening stones shown here not only are large enough, but because of their hardness, will remain flat without the need of dressing (flattening), as is necessary with some other stones. They perform quite nicely for this task. No water or oil should be used on ceramic stones during sharpening.

The Cutting Knife

To begin sharpening with the cutting knife, place the entire blade flat on the medium-grade stone and raise the back of the blade no more than the thickness of a dime or less. With equal pressure on the tip and heel of the blade, and holding the angle constant and steady, slide the blade back and forth while applying pressure on the blade. The object is to remove metal, not tickle the stone. Do both sides of the blade equally.

With a magnifying glass, examine the tip by looking straight onto it with the edge up. If sharpened properly, it should show the blade tapering evenly to the tip. Examine both sides of the blade to ensure the edge is remaining straight. If the blade edge appears to be rounded at the tip, it is because too much pressure is being applied there. This may be straightened with more pressure concentrated on the heel of the blade.

Continue sharpening until all factory grind marks (which appear only on a new knife) are removed and the blade tapers to the tip evenly on both sides with the edge remaining straight.

Looking straight onto the tip of the blade, check that it tapers correctly and evenly on both sides.

Check each side of the blade for straightness.

At this point, what is called a *wire edge* or *burr* should appear evenly along the edge of the blade. It is caused by metal being rolled over the edge of the blade. While a straight, even burr indicates the blade has been prepared for a clean, smooth cutting edge, it needs to be removed.

Remove the burr by using the same sharpening procedure but with very little pressure applied to the blade. Lightly working the burr from one side to the other on the stone will cause the wire edge to fall off, leaving a perfectly straight, sharp edge.

The next step is to take the cutting knife to the ultrafine ceramic stone and continue with the same sharpening procedure, applying pressure on the blade. If done properly, the white ultrafine stone will immediately begin to turn black from metal particles being polished off the blade. When the stone is very black, scrub it clean with an abrasive cleaner and scouring pad. If not removed, a heavy coat of metal particles on the stone will dull the blade rather than polish it.

Check for a burr by running thumb away from, and across the edge.

Continue to polish until the stone no longer removes metal. If a true ultrafine ceramic stone has been employed, no further sharpening preparation for carving should be necessary. By this time the blade should be shiny with a mirror finish.

Finally, check the blade for a burr on the edge or a hook on the tip by running a finger or thumb across the flat of the blade on either side toward the edge. If a dragging or scraping is felt, a burr is present. This can be eliminated by continuing to polish, but with much less pressure. Work the burr from one side to the other until it disappears or finally falls off.

Once a new blade has been sharpened, it only needs to be freshened occasionally on the ultrafine stone during the course of carving. This varies according to the kind of wood being carved and the types of cut being made. Deep and curved cuts will wear an edge faster than shallow, straight cuts. When it seems more pressure is needed for carving, or light reflects off the edge because it is rounded from wear, it's probably a good time to consider refreshing the edge.

The Stab Knife

To sharpen the stab knife, use precisely the same procedure that was used with the cutting knife, with one exception. Because the stab knife functions by impressing or indenting the wood by cutting the fibers and spreading them, the cutting edge is sharpened at a broader angle. This angle, approximately 30 degrees, is already established at the factory.

To begin, bring the knife edge up flat on the established angle on the medium-grade stone and, sliding the blade back and forth on both sides, remove the factory grind marks. Once this is accomplished, employ the same procedure on the ultrafine stone, making sure no burr or wire edge has been created. This done, the knives are ready for carving.

Polish the blade to a mirror finish.

Sharpen the stab knife on the 30-degree angle set at the factory.

4

How to Hold the Knives

ALL HAND TOOLS ARE made to be used and held in a particular fashion. Chip-carving knives are no exception. Though it may feel strange or even awkward at first, with a little practice it will soon become apparent that holding the knives in a correct manner will make carving with them infinitely easier, faster, and safer—and the experience far more pleasant.

Grip the handle with the last three fingers.

First position of the cutting knife.

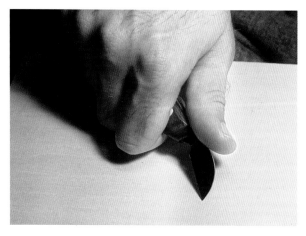

Second position of the cutting knife.

Using the Cutting Edge

The handle of the Premier cutting knife is ergonomically designed to provide hours of comfortable carving. Note that there is a flattened area on either side of the handle (for both right- and left-handed carvers), located on the underside next to the blade.

FIRST HOLDING POSITION

Place the knuckle of the thumb at the end of the flattened area by the blade, with the thumb turned outward from the handle. Positioning the thumb here will provide a fulcrum for the knife to work from while carving. The length of the flattened area allows the thumb to slide easily when it is necessary to raise the blade when carving.

Next, close the hand around the handle, gripping with the last three fingers, not the thumb and first finger. Holding the knife this way will give you more control and power when carving. Rolling the wrist outward will keep the elbow next to the body for better leverage and ensure the knife is drawn toward the body and not across it.

Held properly, the blade should be approximately at a 65-degree angle for carving, with the hand resting on the knuckle of the first finger and the thumb. This is the first position and is the one in which most carving is done.

SECOND HOLDING POSITION

The second position is used primarily when making smaller three-corner or triangular chips and two-corner notches. It is accomplished by placing the thumb knuckle on the spine of the blade at the blade end of the handle. Closing the hand around the handle and placing the hand down on the wood will put the blade at a 65-degree angle opposite that of the first position.

When carving in the first or predominant position, always keep the thumb against the handle, as opposed to carving as one does when peeling potatoes, by drawing the blade toward the thumb. By keeping the thumb against the handle, the correct angle is locked in place and the blade can never cut the thumb by being pulled into it. Also, when the thumb is held against the handle, the knife can be moved only by pulling from the shoulder, giving much greater strength and control while carving.

Additionally, whether carving in the first or second position, some part of the carving hand should always be in contact with the wood. In the first position it will be the thumb bracing, pivoting or sliding on the wood while carving. In the second position, dropping the first finger to the wood will suffice.

Holding the Stab Knife

The stab knife is held by one or two hands perpendicular to the wood with the blade edge toward the carver. It is thrust downward to make an impression deep enough to cut the wood fibers, and rocked on its edge to extend the impression to whatever length desired. This normally is made in a single movement. When using the stab knife, the elbow should be kept close to the body. This will give added leverage and strength from the shoulder.

Wrong position of the thumb, which should always be against the handle when carving.

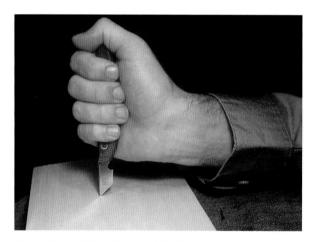

Beginning position of the stab knife.

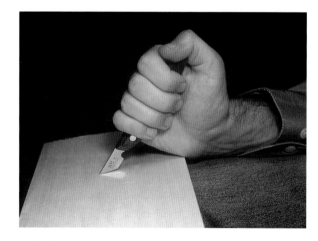

Rock blade down to lengthen the stab cut.

5

HINTS FOR CARVING

TRADITIONALLY, CHIP CARVING was done in a sitting position, and working on the lap. It is still the best way to do this style of carving. To work on a table or bench is to forfeit leverage and strength, and is not recommended. The only exception to this rule would be if the piece being carved is too large to hold on the lap. However, nearly every carving, if not all, will be of a size that can easily be done on the lap.

1. Choose a comfortable chair that allows both feet to set level on the ground. This also makes the lap level, eliminating the need to bend over too far when carving.

2. If artificial lighting is being used, a shaded articulating desk lamp, adjusted below eye level, works well. Any light from above eye level may cause glare, making carving details sometimes difficult to see, and is tiring for the eyes.

Proper position of sitting, holding carving in the lap.

Keep single, shaded light below eye level.

3. In preparing wood for carving, sand the surface with the grain with no finer than 220-grit paper. This allows designs to be more easily drawn directly on the wood. It is also easier to clean off any pencil lines left after carving. Carving off pencil lines in the carving process of removing chips also simplifies cleanup.

4. Before attempting any projects, working on

Design drawn on the wood.

practice boards is a good idea. Using basswood is an excellent choice of wood for these boards. Practicing the rudiments and basic motifs of chip carving will make any project much less formidable and intimidating. Boards measuring in inches 12 × 4 × ⅜ will be easy to hold, manipulate, and control on the lap. When carving, keep the hand holding the board, or work, above or away from the path in which the knife is cutting, for safety reasons.

5. Because the blade is held at a constant angle, the wider the chip, the deeper the cut must be made to relieve it. Conversely, a small or narrow chip needs only the tip of the blade to remove it. It is common for a novice to cut much deeper than necessary to remove chips. This practice often will relieve wood not intended to be removed. It is very important not to cut any deeper than necessary. However, this recommendation includes a slight undercutting of chips to ensure they're being released with normal, single-cut passes with the knife.

Small chips need only the tip of the blade to remove them.

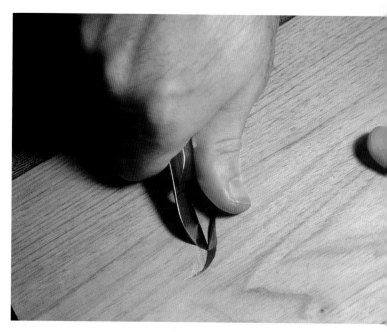

A slight undercut on relieving chip removes it from the wood.

Removing top half of large chip.

Removing bottom half of chip without changing blade angle.

6. There are occasions when a chip may be too large to remove in a single pass. In this case, cut as normal, removing the top half of the chip. This will make clearly visible how deep to cut to remove the remainder of the chip. Often, the novice carver has a tendency to tilt the blade at a steeper angle to clear the chip. This habit leaves additional wood on the side walls of the chipped area and makes the chip too deep. Whenever it takes more than a single pass to remove a chip, be sure the blade is held at the same angle for subsequent cuts.

7. For consistently clean and good-looking results in carving, with a few exceptions, hold the blade at a 65-degree angle. Cutting too shallow an angle makes the carving appear flat and lifeless because a lack of shadows will not show the carving. Cutting too steep an angle will make it difficult, if not impossible, to remove chips, and render any ridges in the design weak.

Blade angle—(1) wrong, shallow—(2) wrong, deep—(3) correct 65-degree angle.

8. When making straight line cuts, let the hand ride on the thumb and the knuckle of the first finger as it guides the knife through the wood. Straight lines can be made quite easily if focus is concentrated about a half-inch in front of the blade (as shown by the x mark in the photo at right) instead of on the blade itself, letting the eye "pull" the blade.

9. The use of a straight edge to assist in cutting a straight line is not recommended. A tool in each hand dramatically increases the possibility of an error, particularly if the straight edge inadvertently moves. It is not wise to divide one's attention when carving.

10. The use of a razor blade or razor knife for carving is also not recommended. This tool is not designed to carve wood, a practice fraught with potential problems. A carving knife sharpened properly will perform far more dependably, with its handle specifically designed for comfort, security, and safety. Any scoring of the wood, if at all necessary, can be done quite easily and neatly with the cutting knife.

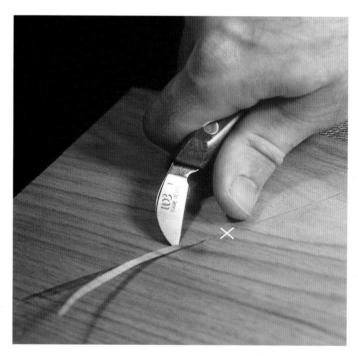

Cutting a straight line.

11. When making curved cuts, raise the blade to a more vertical position while maintaining the 65-degree cutting angle. This maneuver will reduce the amount of blade edge in the wood, allowing clean, smooth cuts to be made in curves. The tighter the curve, the higher the blade will need to be raised.

12. The Premier cutting knife, with its thin tapering blade tempered for toughness, will carve very well for many years with proper care. However, if a chip does not release from the wood cleanly, it is because all the fibers have not been severed. While it may be tempting to pry the chip out, the blade is not designed to

Normal cutting position of knife.

Blade raised to make smooth, curved cuts.

function in this manner, and prying with it runs the risk of breaking off the tip. If a chip does not release freely, cut it loose, do not pry.

13. When sharpening a compass lead, sharpen on an angle on one side only. Use a compass point with a shoulder to minimize the size of the hole made in the wood. To remove the hole made by the compass point, put a drop of water on it, which will swell the wood fibers back. When the wood dries, sand lightly over where the water was placed.

14. With few exceptions, when carving, make the first cut of a new chip away from ones already carved. This will help prevent wood not intended to be removed from splitting. If any wood breaks out and needs to be glued back, a dab of white glue will do nicely. Be careful not to get any on the surface, as it will leave a clear spot if stain is later used.

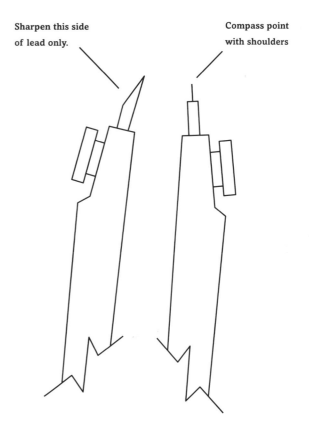

Sharpen this side of lead only.

Compass point with shoulders

Make first cut of new chip away from ones already carved.

15. When two chips of the same configuration are next to each other and come to a point, as is common at the center of a rosette, carve one all the way to the center of the rosette and hold the other short of the center (see the photo on page 28). This will prevent the creation of ridges that are too thin and risk being undercut and easily broken out, particularly when carving cross-grain. Under these conditions it mayalso be necessary to roll the knife blade above the normal 65-degree angle to prevent excessive undercutting.

16. The term "stacking" refers to the method of removing the chips of fan and similar motifs in such a manner as to minimize the possibility of splitting out wood not intended to be removed. As an example, rather than bringing all chips of a "four-chip fan" to the same point, only the two outside chips are brought to the center point to define the motif. The two inside chips are held short, or "stacked" just above the center point of the outside chips. Visually, it appears that all four chips are brought to the same point.

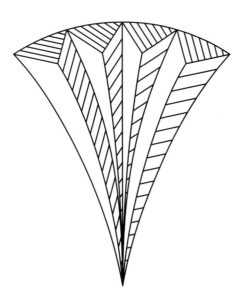

Four-chip fan. Note two inner chips are held short of the tip.

First cut of fan motif is a stop cut on top.

Second cuts of fan motif. Note the blade is nearly out of the wood at narrow end of the chip.

Note interior chip cuts stop short of end of pattern.

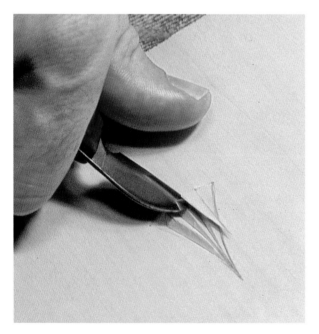

Relieving interior chip short of end of pattern.

Relieving exterior chip extending to end of pattern.

17. While some rosettes and other motifs are attractive when carved in a negative attitude with all the wood removed within, it is not a good idea to overcarve an entire composition. Leave visual breathing space. Simplicity often makes the best statement.

Note all the right-hand chips go to the center; the left-hand chips are held short.

6

LAYING OUT AND TRANSFERRING PATTERNS

LAYING OUT ALL THE BASIC lines of a design ensures that the finished work will be proportionally correct and visually balanced. Whether the shape of the piece to be carved is round or square, begin by quartering it. This will locate the exact center and provide the basis for all other divisions. If the design is entirely geometric, all or most of it can be easily drawn directly onto the wood with the aid of a ruler and compass.

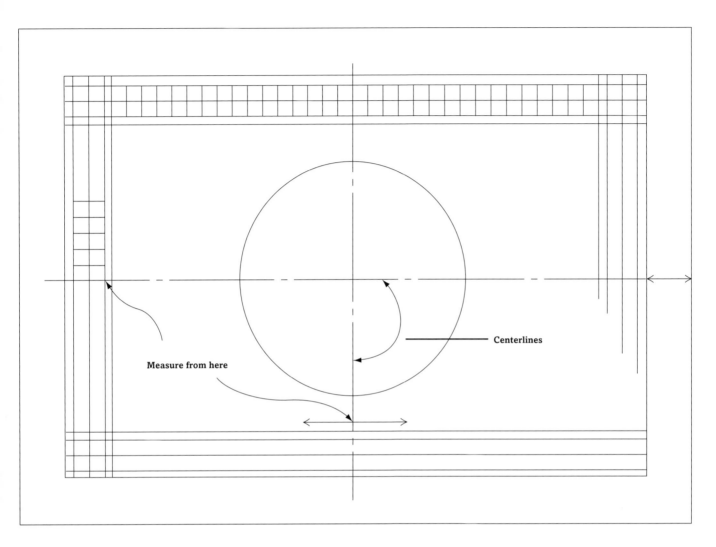

Centerlines

Measure from here

Lay out border lines in millimeters, quarter the carving, and measure pattern from centerlines for equal spacing.

Use graphite paper under tracing paper to transfer free-form designs onto wood.

Tracing Patterns onto the Wood

When nongeometric designs and patterns such as those representing foliage are to be transferred, they are best drawn on tracing paper first. Being able to see through the paper allows the pattern to be positioned perfectly on the wood. Hold the paper in place with removable tape. Place graphite paper between the wood and the tracing paper, and, with a nonmarking stylus to maintain the integrity of the original design, trace the pattern onto the wood. The use of carbon paper should be avoided because the colored wax transmitted from this material can permanently stain the wood.

ADHESIVE IS NOT RECOMMENDED

It is not recommended to glue the pattern onto the wood and carve through the paper. While this may appear to be a shortcut as one prepares to carve, it has serious drawbacks. It is impossible to see through the paper to position it properly on the wood or during the process of carving. While carving, wood may split or be cut that was not intended to be removed. Even if transparent paper is used, the same result may occur and not be discovered until the paper is removed. Having the paper move or come loose during carving is also a concern. Removing adhesive after the paper is lifted is not only bothersome, but raises the possibility of damaging the carving.

7

BORDERS

BORDERS ARE THE FRAMEWORK of a carving composition. They may also represent the entire composition. From a single line to elaborate and multiple combinations, borders set the tone of and complement a carving, much as does the frame of a picture.

Traditionally in chip carving, the three-cornered or triangular chip in various positions and combinations provided many or most of the borders commonly used. While the three-cornered chip is versatile, many other possibilities exist, of which a few are shown in this section. Their dimensions and proportions will vary according to the border selected, the piece being carved, and its size. However, for most household pieces—from boxes to plates utilizing various lace borders or those of the three-cornered chip—working in dimensional increments of four millimeters will do nicely. It's large enough to show the chip well and small enough to carve easily.

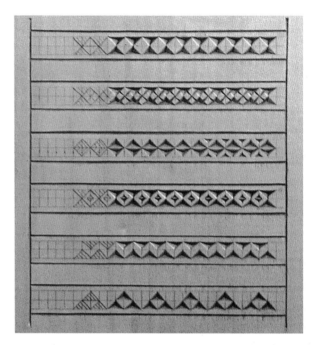

Borders made from same three-cornered chip. (top to bottom): positive diamond, flower, negative diamond, double diamond, zigzag, pyramid.

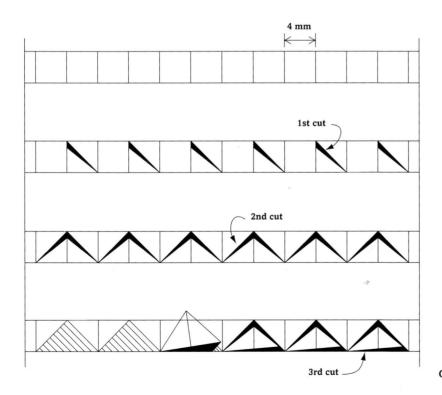

Order of cuts for three-cornered chip.

Three-Cornered Chip

To begin, hold the cutting knife in the first position. Place the tip at the corner of a square and raise the blade up so that it forms a V without losing the 65-degree cutting angle. Maintaining the 65-degree angle, thrust (not draw) the knife straight into the wood to the opposite corner of the square. In the first position, the thumb should always be against the handle of the knife and touching the work.

Next, turn the work 180 degrees and switch the cutting knife to the second position. Place the tip at the same corner as when the first cut was made and thrust to the opposite corner of the square next to the original square. In the second position, the first finger is extended to be in touch with the work. In chip carving, some part of the carving hand is always touching the wood in order that the carver has a tactile relationship with the work.

For the third cut, which frees the chip completely, switch the knife back to the first position without turning the work. Place the tip of the blade on the uncut side of the chip. Because the length of the base (the third cut) is longer than the two sides, the third and relieving cut is made with a slicing motion. Draw the blade while pressing down (inserting) until the knife has run the entire third side. If executed correctly, the chip will pop right out. Upon examination, note how the three sides of the chip automatically meet at the center at the bottom of the chip.

First cut of a three-cornered chip, knife held in first position.

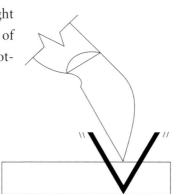

Correct angle of cutting knife when making three-cornered chip.

65 degrees

Second cut of a three-cornered chip, knife in second position.

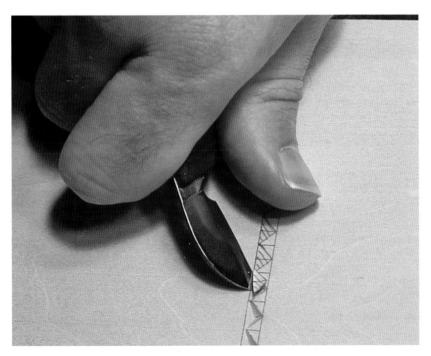

Third and relieving cut for a three-cornered chip, knife in first position.

Lace Border

The pattern of the lace border is not exlusively for chip carving. It has been known by other names and used for centuries in other disciplines from architecture to ironwork. Easily drawn, its appeal is found in its alternating large and small, curved and diamond-shaped motifs. In chip carving, it may be carved in a single, double, or triple border form.

To carve a lace border, as in all chip carving, it is not necessary to draw a line for every cut to be made. A good number of cuts will be made by eye measure alone. Also, all cuts here will be made with the knife in the first position. Make the first cut on the line and the second (relieving) cut underneath the arch of the first. Note the center of this chip is wider than its ends. The depth of the knife must be adjusted to this change while carving to avoid cutting too deeply and taking out wood not intended to be removed.

Single, double, and triple lace borders.

Single ——————

Double ——————

Triple ——————

First chip of
lace border.

Second chip of
lace border.

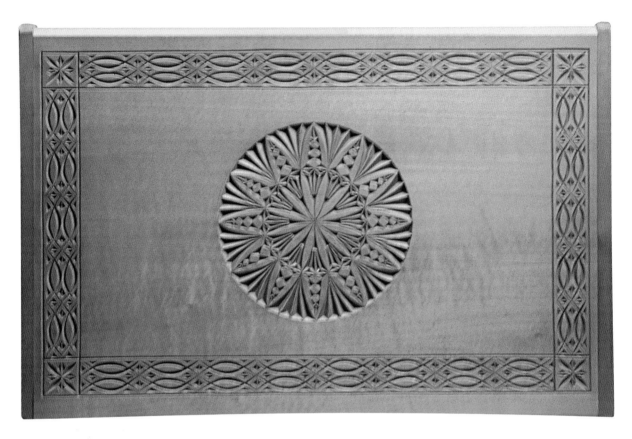

12³/₄" and 8¹/₄" box lid, basswood
with double lace border and lace
rosette.

Rope Border

The rope border is like the lace border with its two-cut chip and the center wider than the ends. This variation in the chip width mimics visually the twist of real rope, to which any sailor will attest. Like the lace border, the variation of width in the chip gives an appearance of a third dimension.

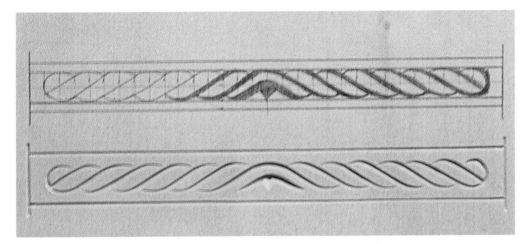

Layout for the rope border.

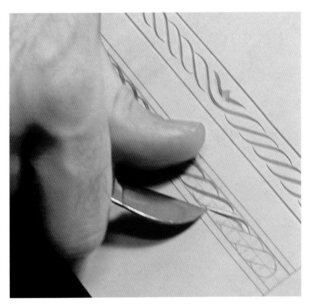

Carving the rope border.

12³/₄" x 8¹/₄" box lid, basswood with rope border, rosette, and single-line grid.

Gothic Border

This border is so named for its popularity in northern European Gothic architecture. It can be found in stonework as well as wood. The charm and appeal of this border is the repeating movement of a geometric form centered with a stylized flower, all within another geometric form. It has a true three-dimensional appearance.

To minimize the risk of splitting the wood while carving, remove all three-cornered chips first. Secondly, remove chips around the flower in the order indicated in the drawing. The last chips to be removed are the notch cuts, used to create the center flower. Again, to minimize splitting, cut the cross-grain notches first.

Layout for the Gothic border.

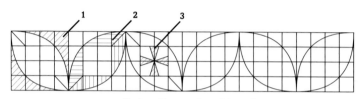

Order of removing chips of a Gothic border.

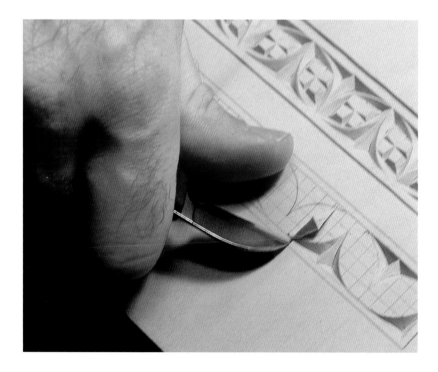

Removing three-cornered chips first from Gothic border.

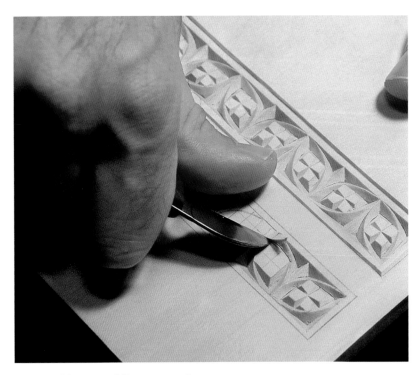

Remove chips around flower second.

Make notches in flower last.

12³/₄" x 8¹/₄" box lid, basswood with Gothic border and rosette adapted from the rose window of cathedral in Amiens, France, 1200 C.E.

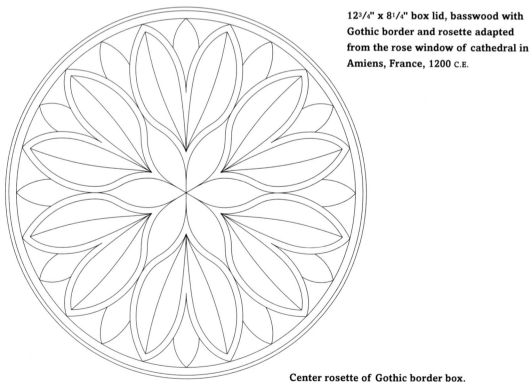

Center rosette of Gothic border box.

Borders: (top to bottom) three-cornered chip (first three), button, button-and-dart, cable, pyramid, ribbon, egg-and-dart.

Borders: (top to bottom) flower, heart, garland, large flower, paisley.

Quarter section for multiple borders on a plate.

10" plate, basswood with multiple borders.

12" x 18" wall plaque with garland border, positive image, and incised motifs.

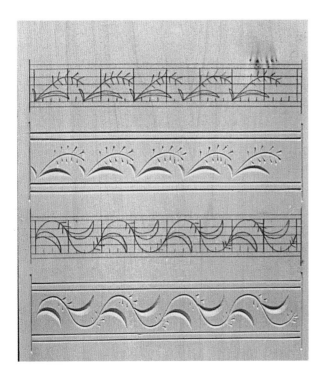

Floral and vine borders

14" plate, basswood with scallop, ribon, and heart borders.

8" plate, basswood with scalloped and zigzag borders. Note accents made with stab knife.

GRIDS

A GRID DESIGN is usually employed to decorate or add texture to larger areas such as panels on cabinets and chests or box lids with a repeating, geometric pattern. This may be accomplished with simple diagonal lines alone, or with a more elaborate combination of motifs. The key is that the motif is repetitive, giving a visual rhythm to the overall design.

While some grid designs are oriented to the square, most grids have a more diagonal attitude. Diagonal lines tend to visually extend outward, broadening a carving's appearance. Diagonal lines also express energy and movement. Using alternating, opposite motifs (such as large and small, angled and round, etc.) is a technique that often adds interest to a design. Opposites define each other by making the other more apparent.

Another function of a grid is to add background texture to a composition that has other design components such as a border and a center theme rosette. A grid used in this way often will visually tie the components together. In this instance, it is best not to select an elaborate or busy style of grid that may overpower or dominate the main theme and other components. A simple diagonal line grid will do nicely.

Line grid accented with stab knife.

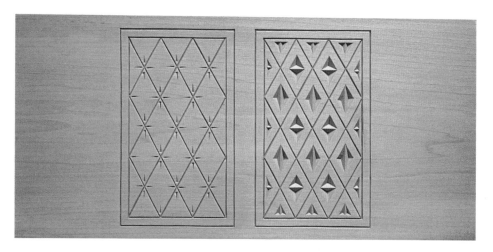

Line grid accented with negative diamonds.

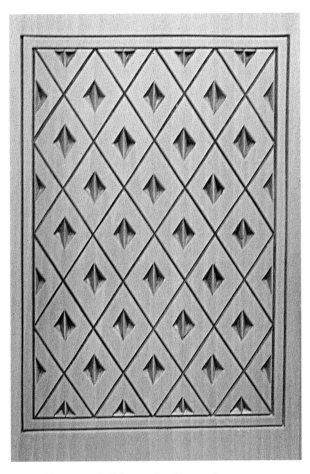

Line grid accented with negative diamonds.

Floral grid.

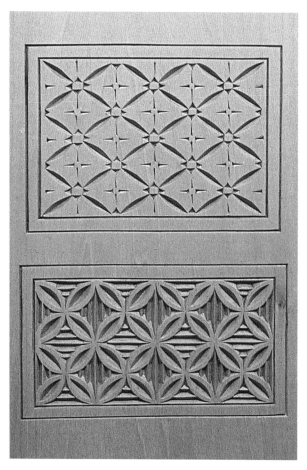

Scalloped and floral grids.

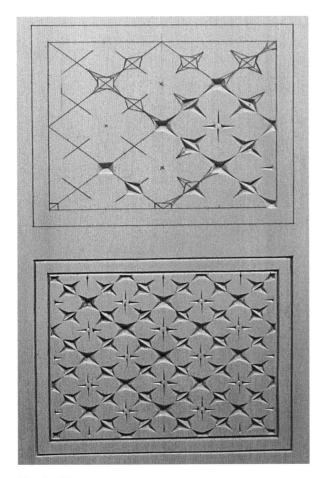

Floral grids.

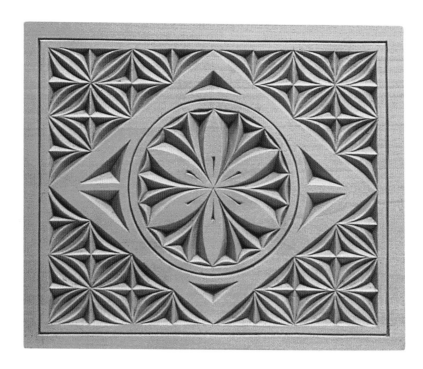

7" x 5³/₄" box lid, basswood with incised grid and rosette with diamond motif.

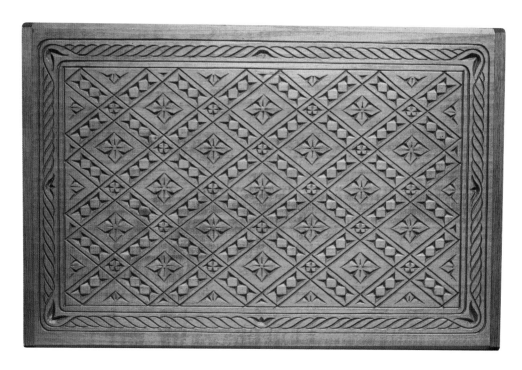

12³/₄" x 8¹/₄" box lid, basswood with floral and diamond grid and rope border.

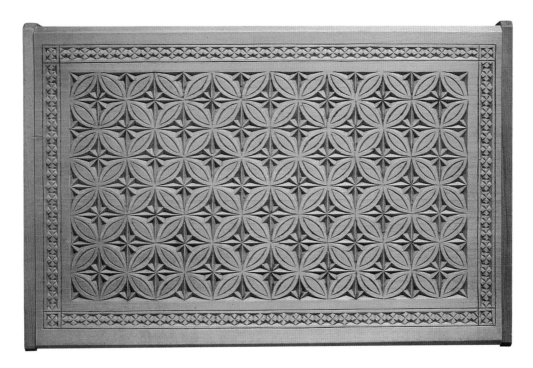

12³/₄" x 8¹/₄" box lid, basswood with circles in squares grid and floral border.

12³/₄" x 8¹/₄" box lid, basswood with line grid, rope border, and Old English "H".

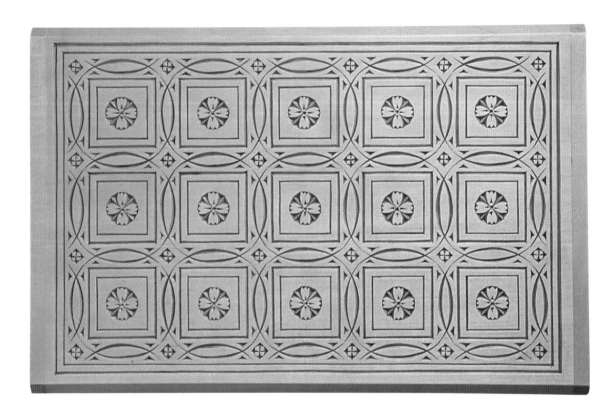

12³/₄" x 8¹/₄" box lid, basswood with squares-in-circles grid and double line border.

9

ROSETTES

THE DESIGN MOTIF known as a rosette has ancient origins and may be found in many disciplines of art as well as architecture. This designation refers to ornamentation resembling a rose, or a design having a generally circular combination of parts. These parts are equal divisions of a circle normally numbering from three to twelve and have often symbolically represented the sacred and the mystical.

In chip carving, these equal divisions are easily made with just a compass and ruler as illustrated. When drawing rosettes, as with all other designs, accuracy is paramount. Make sure the compass lead is sharp (sharpen on the outward side only) and all lines are thin, limiting the possibility of design variation. Also, give attention to placing the compass point precisely.

By their nature, rosettes offer an almost unlimited variety of design possibilities. In some instances, a single design may be carved as either negative or positive. Because of their design possibilities, rosettes often are employed as the center or central focal point of chip-carved compositions. They may also comprise the entire composition.

Negative and positive rosettes from same design.

Design and carving to twelve-point rosette.

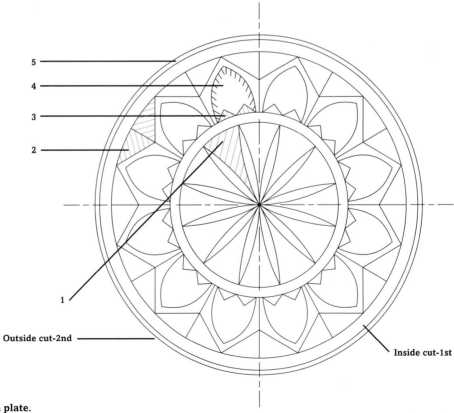

Cuts for borders and design on plate.

Three-point rosettes.

Three-Point Rosette

DRAWING A TRIGON OR TRIANGLE

1. Draw a vertical line (A-2)
2. Make a circle at point 1.
3. Using the same compass opening, place compass at point 2 and strike points B and C.
4. Points A, B, and C form an equilateral triangle.

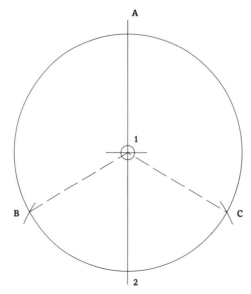

Four-Point Rosette

DRAWING A TETRAGON

1. Draw a horizontal line (2-3).
2. Make a circle at point 1.
3. Open compass larger than original radius. Set new compass opening at points 2 and 3 and strike intersections, establishing points A and B.
4. A line drawn from points A and B will bisect original line, forming right angles, and divide circle into four equal parts.

Four-point rosettes.

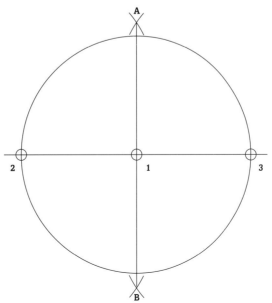

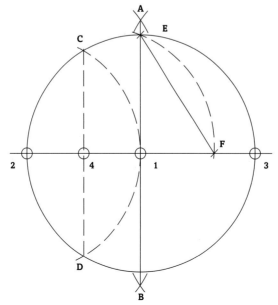

Five-point rosettes.

Five-Point Rosette

DRAWING A PENTAGON

1. Draw a horizontal line (2-3).
2. Make a circle at point 1.
3. Using the same compass opening, set compass at point 2 and strike points C and D.
4. Draw line C-D, establishing point 4.
5. Open compass larger than original radius. Set new compass opening at points 2 and 3 and strike intersections, establishing line A-B and point E.
6. Set compass opening from point 4 to point E and draw arch E-F.
7. Set compass opening at E-F. This setting is one fifth of the circumference, dividing the circle into five equal parts.

Six-Point Rosette

DRAWING A HEXAGON

1. Draw a horizontal line (2-5)
2. Make a circle at point 1.
3. Using the same compass opening, set compass at point 2 and strike points 3 and 7.
4. Set compass at point 3 and repeat until returning to point 2. This will divide the circle into six equal parts.

Six-point rosettes.

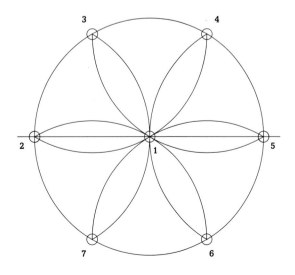

Seven-point rosettes.

Seven-Point Rosette

DRAWING A HEPTAGON

1. Draw a horizontal line (2-3)
2. Make a circle at point 1.
3. Using the same compass opening, set compass at point 2 and strike points A and B.
4. Draw line A-B, establishing point C.
5. Set compass opening at A-C. This setting is one seventh of the circumference, dividing the circle into seven equal parts.

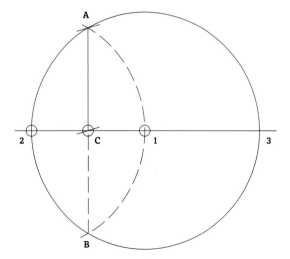

Eight-Point Rosette

DRAWING AN OCTAGON

1. Draw a horizontal line (2-3).
2. Make a circle at point 1.
3. Open compass larger than original radius. Set new compass opening at points 2 and 3 and strike intersections A and B, establishing points 4 and 5.
4. Reduce compass opening to smaller than original radius. Set compass at point 2 and strike between 2-A and 2-B. Repeat at points 3, 4, and 5. This will establish intersections C, D, E, and F.
5. Lines drawn from points A-B, C-E, and D-F will complete the division of the circle into eight equal parts.

Eight-point rosettes.

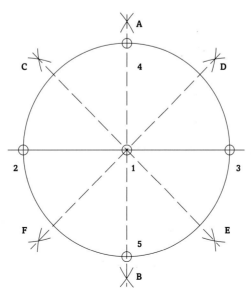

Nine-point rosettes.

Nine-Point Rosette

DRAWING A NONOGON OR ENNEAGON

1. Draw a vertical line (2-3)
2. Make a circle at point 1.
3. Using the same compass opening, set compass at point 2 and strike points 4 and 5. Repeat at point 3 and strike points 6 and 7.
4. Draw lines 2-6, 2-7, 3-4, 3-5, 4-5, 4-7, 6-7, and 5-6. This will establish points A, B, C, and D.
5. Set compass from point A to point D and draw an arc. Using the same compass setting, repeat drawing arcs at points B and C.
6. Points (clockwise) 2, G, H, 7, J, K, 6, E, and F will divide the circle into nine equal parts.

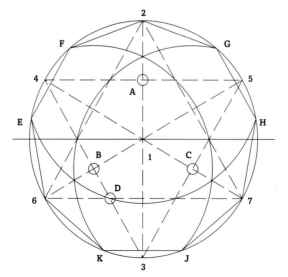

Ten-Point Rosette

DRAWING A DECAGON

1. Draw a vertical line (A-2).
2. Make a circle at point 1.
3. Repeat procedure for five-point rosette, establishing points A, B, C, D, and E.
4. Using the same compass openings, set compass at point 2 and repeat step 3, establishing points F, G, H, and J. This will complete the division of the circle into ten equal parts.

Ten-point rosettes.

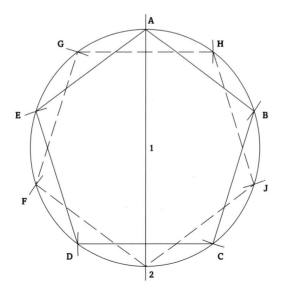

Twelve-point rosettes.

Twelve-Point Rosette

DRAWING A DODECAGON

1. Repeat procedure for six-point rosette.
2. Bisect line A-B, establishing line 2-3.
3. Using the same compass opening, set compass at point 2 and repeat step 1. This will complete the division of the circle into twelve equal parts.

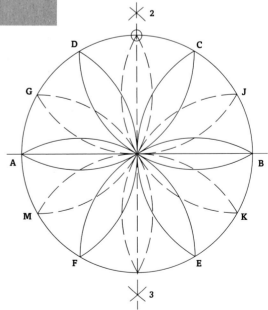

Swirl rosette.

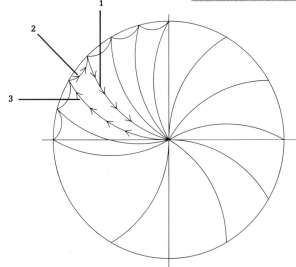

Negative rosette.

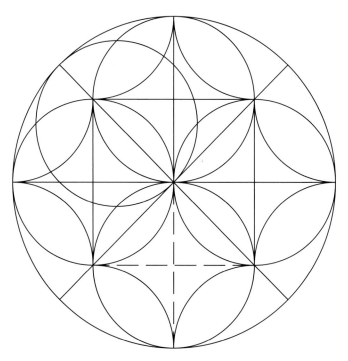

Lace rosette.

Four-point rosette

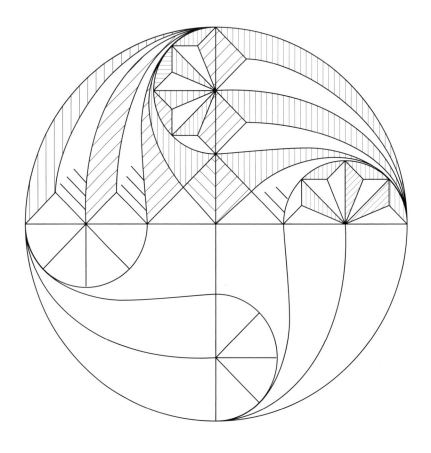

Compass rose.

Six-point rosette, butternut.

12³/₄" x 8¹/₄" box lid, basswood with lace border and four-point rosette in process of carving.

6" plate with six-point rosette.

6" plate with interlocking circles rosette.

6" hexagon plate with six-point rosette.

8" plate with six-point rosette and star.

6" plate with five-point rosette.

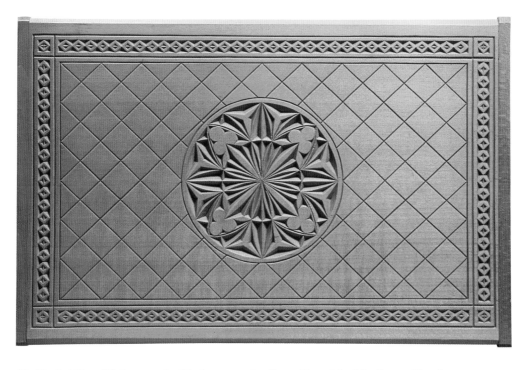

12³/₄" x 8¹/₄" box lid, basswood with clover rosette, line grid, and double diamond border.

14" plate, basswood with paisley rosette and incised floral border.

8" plate with six-point rosette and star.

10

FREE-FORM DESIGN

FREE-FORM CHIP CARVING is a style that generally steers away from geometrical design. It is commonly used to depict natural forms such as animals, birds, flowers, and foliage. The subject may be outlined with a simple, incised groove or be more elaborately carved by defining specific parts of a subject such as carving the individual feathers of a bird.

Free-form motifs can be realistic or fanciful, symmetrical or irregular, simple or ornate. They can be combined with other design elements such as geometrical components and lettering. They differ from positive-image motifs in one major way. While positive images are created by carving away the background to produce a design, free-form designs are incised into the wood. What is cut out is the design.

Outlining an Image

When outlining free-form patterns, as is often done to define an image, a three-dimensional and livelier attitude is easily imparted by varying the width of the chip or line defining the image.

Because natural forms can be interpreted in so many different ways, free-form motifs offer a wonderful opportunity for a variety of design possibilities.

Vary width of outlining chip the three-dimensional effect.

Dividing and accent devices.

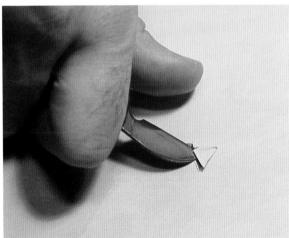

To make a six-point incised star, cut an equilateral triangle.

Step two: notch each side equally.

Dividing and accent devices.

Edelweiss 5".

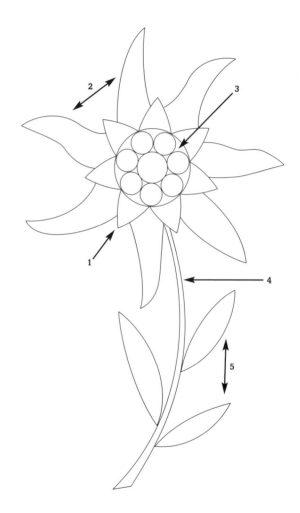

Order for removing chips of edelweiss.

Dandelion 4".

Thistle 3".

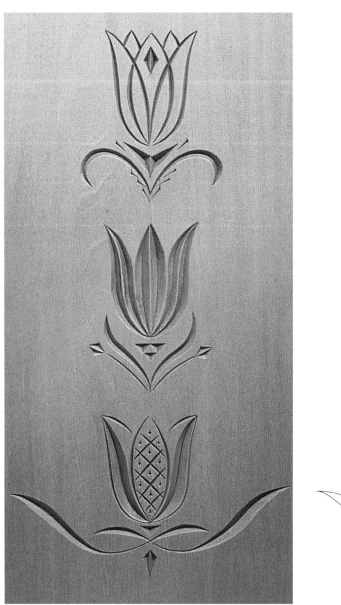

Three stylized tulips.

Symmetrical bouquet 6" x 12".

8" plate with floral motif, zigzag, and scalloped border.

Front panel of box, basswood, 12" x 5" with rosette and floral motif.

12³/₄" x 8¹/₄" box lid, basswood with
rosette and floral motif.

16" x 5" needle box lid, basswood with rosette and floral motif.

10" plate, basswood with star and positive image leaf border.

14" plate, basswood with owl and leaves.

Lovebirds.

11

POSITIVE IMAGE DESIGN

GENERALLY SPEAKING, any chip carving that produces a recognizable form in relief, i.e., not incised, such as a bird, animal, or flower, would be classified as having a positive image. In traditional chip carving, certain motifs such as six- and twelve-point rosettes, automatically, when drawn, produce stylized floral patterns that may be carved by removing the background, making the floral pattern a positive image. This, however, is more a result of the geometric characteristics of rosettes than of having an original intention to create a positive image, particularly one that cannot be drawn geometrically.

Creating a positive image is a whole new dimension added to traditional chip carving. Using chip-carving techniques, the background area of a piece is removed, producing a style closer to what is more commonly recognized as relief carving. This style of chip carving is particularly effective when creating foliage within geometric shapes such as circles, triangles, etc., but is equally effective using non-geometric shapes and other natural forms. The concept of positive images extends and expands the parameters of chip carving to dimensions previously not incorporated in traditional design, allowing carvers an opportunity for broader artistic expression.

12" plate, basswood stained with leaf and diamond border.

6" plate, basswood stained with oak leaf trefoil.

8" plate, basswood stained with trefoil and leaf border.

Box panel 5¹/₂" x 4", basswood with leaf motif.

10" plate,
basswood
with leaf
and diamond
border, six-point
rosette center.

10" plate,
basswood
with leaf and
fan border,
twelve-point
rosette center.

napkin holder
6" with basswood
leaf and
branches.

Bellows 17" x 8",
butternut with
leaf border,
four-point
rosette center.

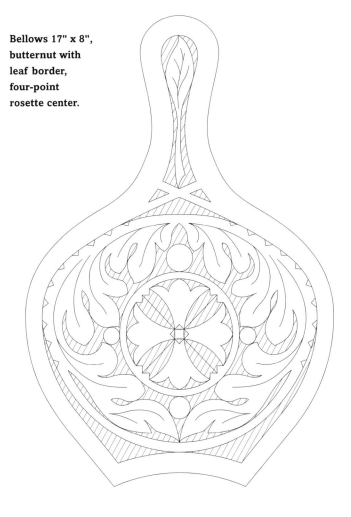

Mirror 14" x 6¹/₂", basswood with leaf and berry borderaround diamond center.

13" x 9" basswood wall clock with leaf and bird motifs.

10" plate, basswood with leaf and flower border, six-point rosette center.

12" plate, basswood stained with double-beaded rim, foliated border and geometric center motifs.

10" plate, basswood with Baroque style leaf.

17" x 9" mantel clock , butternut stained showing leaf and cable motif.

Mantel clock, side view.

14" plate, basswood with leaf and diamond, ribbon, and tulip borders, star and leaf center

12

Lettering

CARVING LETTERS is an ancient practice and tradition. From simple initials and names on gift pieces to elaborate exterior building adornment in wood or stone, the carving of initials, names, dates, mottoes, prayers, quotations, memorials, and more has played an important part in human and artistic expression.

In woods commonly used for chip carving, the incising method is the fastest and easiest way to execute lettering. The techniques employed are the same as in all other chip, carving with a few additional guidelines for selecting a font and spacing.

Guidelines for Lettering

Art demands flexibility. Because there are always exceptions, it is best to consider the following as guidelines, and not as hard-and-fast rules. For example, most modern Arabic lettering is based on the classical Roman font, which stipulates for maximum legibility that the vertical members of a letter be wider than the horizontal ones in approximately a 2:1 ratio. But because of its nature, the letter N reverses this guideline by having its vertical strokes (or legs) narrow instead of wide, to avoid an otherwise clumsy appearance.

Similarly, the guidelines given here for spacing are mostly for viewing lettering close up, as would be commonly done on a personal piece such as a jewelry box. But if the lettering is to be generally viewed from a distance (as it may be within a cathedral or similar edifice), the letters would not only be proportionally larger but would also be spaced a bit further apart because lines tend to converge when seen from a distance. Under this condition, spacing the letters farther apart renders the words more legible.

LAYING OUT THE LETTERING

Carving technique aside, the secret to excellent lettering is in the layout. The most important part of laying out letters is spacing. The most common error made in spacing is placing the letters too far apart, which becomes more pronounced when the letters are carved. Shadow depth and the three-dimensional aspect of carved letters accentuate all that is superior and inferior.

Unless there is some artistic reason for an exaggerated separation of the letters in words or names, it normally is best not to do so. As an example, the letters that form the words on this page are close

enough together as not to be seen individually but read as part of a whole. We read words, not letters. Spreading the letters too far apart forces the eye to jump back and forth in an effort to tie them together into words, making reading difficult and annoying.

There are two methods of spacing or adjusting letters within a word. One is mechanical, as produced in print work. This method, while quite readable, does not take into account that all letters do not inherently fit well together or space equally with other letters. This becomes more obvious as letter size increases.

The other method of spacing is artistic, which allows letters within a word to be adjusted closer together or farther apart as needed, for visual compatibility, creating spatial balance of light and dark between all letters within words, whatever they may be.

To illustrate the difference between these two methods of spacing, consider the letters A and V in a Roman font. When typeset mechanically, a notable gap exists between them. The result of the artistic approach is far more pleasing, having the two letters placed closer together. Drawing words and names out first on tracing paper simplifies the process of adjusting the letters artistically.

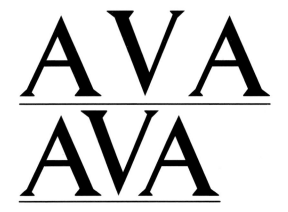

CHECKING THE LETTER SPACING

There are several ways to check for proper spacing. Viewing letters by squinting until the letters become blurred will reveal whether the space between the letters is proportionally balanced. The same effect can be obtained by looking through the back side of the tracing paper held up to a light. The paper blurs the letters and the eye sees only shapes, revealing whether they are properly spaced. Another method is to view the lettering in a mirror. Because we do not normally read words in reverse, the letters lose their cognitive association and what remains is only the spacing of light and dark. Once the lettering is satisfactorily spaced, it (or any other drawing) can be easily transferred to wood by tracing it with a stylus and placing graphite paper between the tracing paper and the wood.

While an artistic approach rather than a mechanical one achieves the best letter-spacing results, the following recommendations will help determine the actual distance between letters. Keep in mind (as mentioned earlier) that there will be variations between letters, and from one font to another.

Considering that serifs (the small flairs or points at the top and bottom of a letter) are an integral part of the letter, the space between letters is one-half the width of the vertical stroke or leg. For example, if the vertical stroke of H is ¼-inch wide, the next letter would be spaced ⅛-inch away.

The space between words is one-half the height of the capital letter of any particular font. The space between the period at the end of a sentence and the first letter of the next sentence is the full height of the capital. This represents double spacing as prac-ticed in typing. The space between lines of words is also one-half the height of the capital. For example, if the capital of a particular type is 1½ inches high, the top of the capitals on the next line will be ¾ inches below the first line.

Choosing a Font

When choosing a font, consider the design that it will accompany, the occasion, and where and how it will be seen. If a selected font has both an upper and lowercase, it is normally best to use them together as originally intended. Some fonts, such as Old English, have very ornate capitals. If only the capitals were to be used in this style, the words would become difficult, if not impossible to read.

While there are many typefaces or fonts from which to choose, they do not all lend themselves easily to carving. Illustrated in this section are five typefaces quite different from each other, all having their own character and all pleasing to carve.

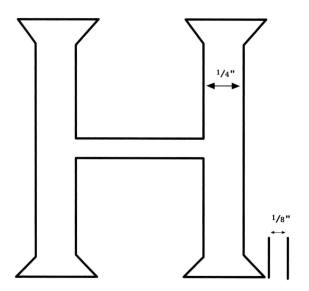

Classic Roman

There are a number of Roman-style fonts. This one is quite basic, easy to carve, and very legible. Unlike some other Roman fonts, Classic Roman has only uppercase letters. Its simple form fits well with many designs.

A–L Roman.

M–W Roman.

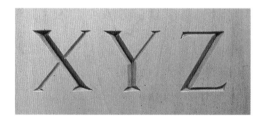

X–Z Roman.

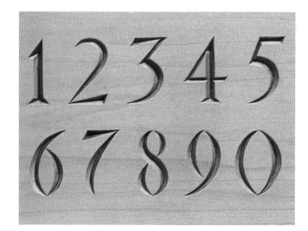

Roman numbers.

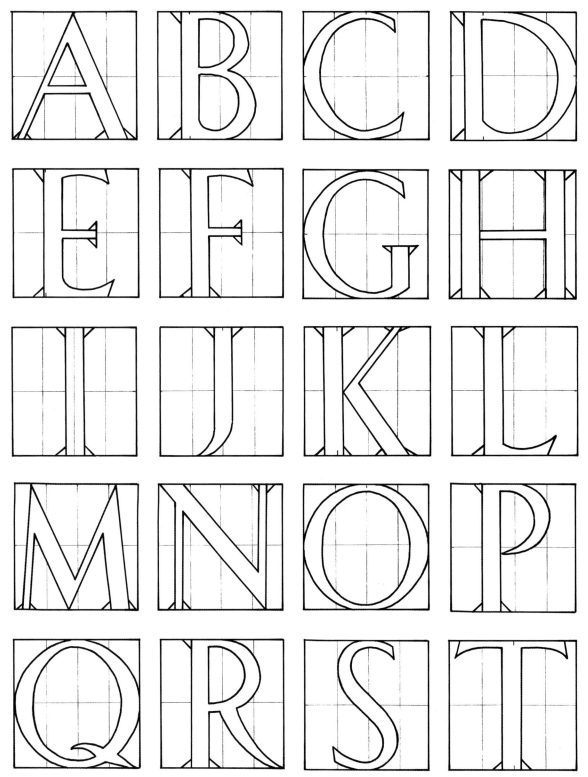

A–T Roman.

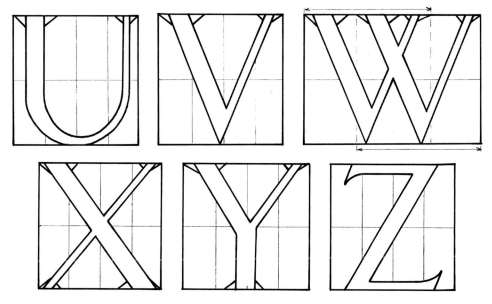

U–Z Roman.

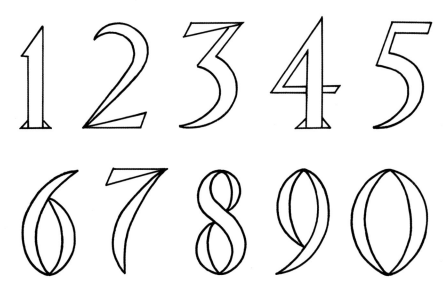

Roman numbers.

Old English

This strong and bold-style typeface with its several variations is known by other names, including Old German, Gothic, Black Letter, and Fraktur. The capitals show very well alone or as initials, but when Old English is selected for names or words, both upper and lowercases must be used for legibility. Using only the capitals of this font is artistically incorrect.

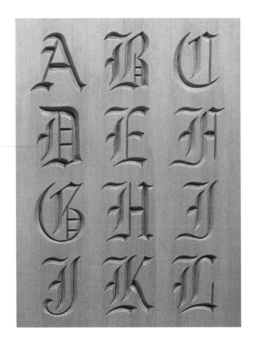

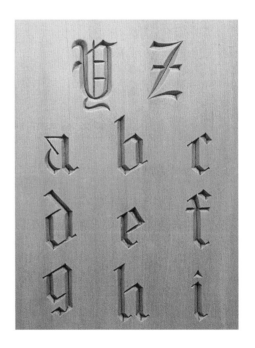

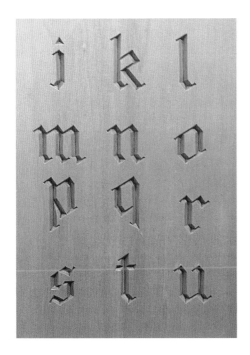

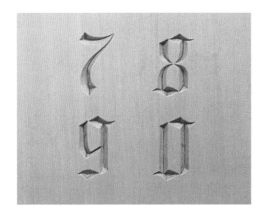

A–T Old English caps.

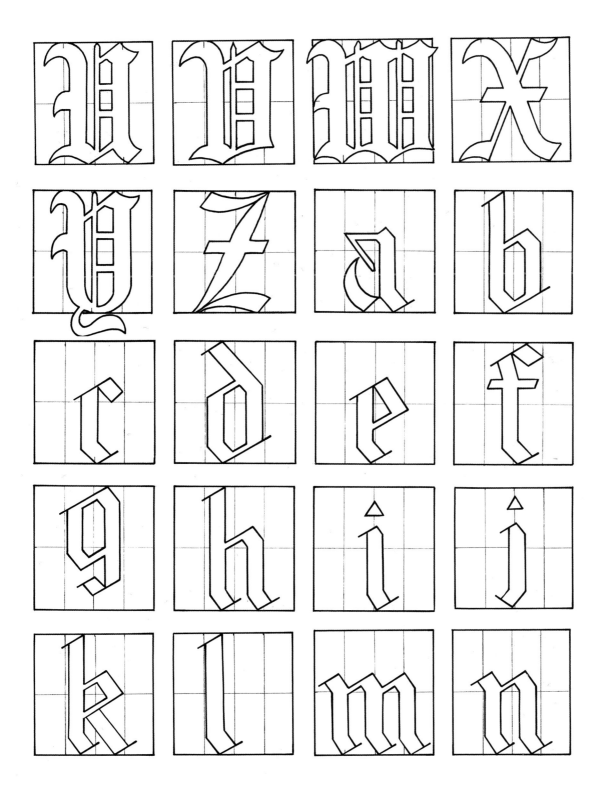

U–Z Old English caps, A–N lowercase.

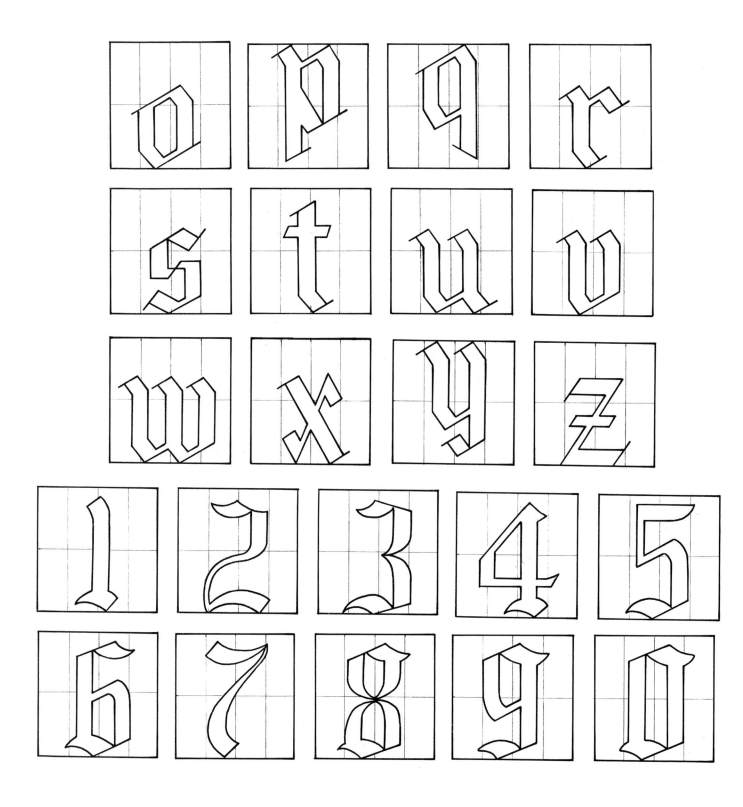

O–Z Old English lowercase, numbers.

Spencerian Script

Script lettering is a very fancy and flowing style that can blend nicely with a design of similar form, or be an actual part of it. Of all the script forms, Spencerian script is one of the easier to carve and lends itself very well to designing monograms.

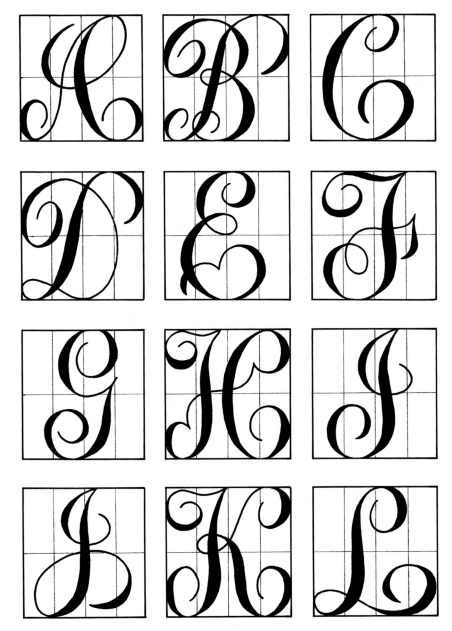

Script A–L.

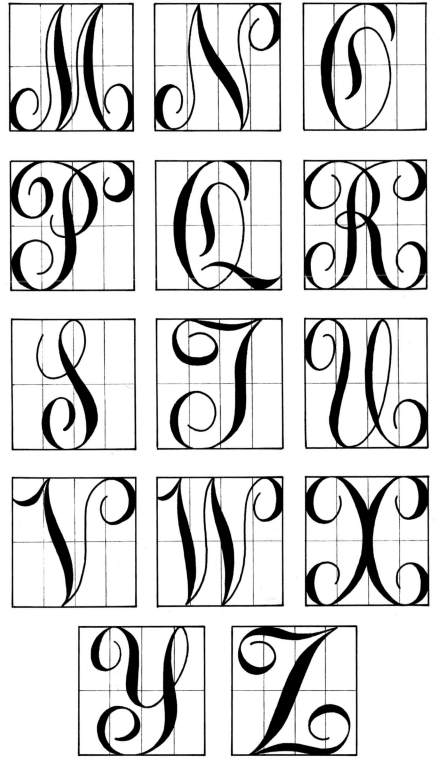

Script M–Z.

Becker

The Becker font is a cross between the Roman and Old English styles. It has a medieval flavor to it with good anatomy, as well. This is another style that calls for both upper and lowercases, though it's a bit more flexible than Old English.

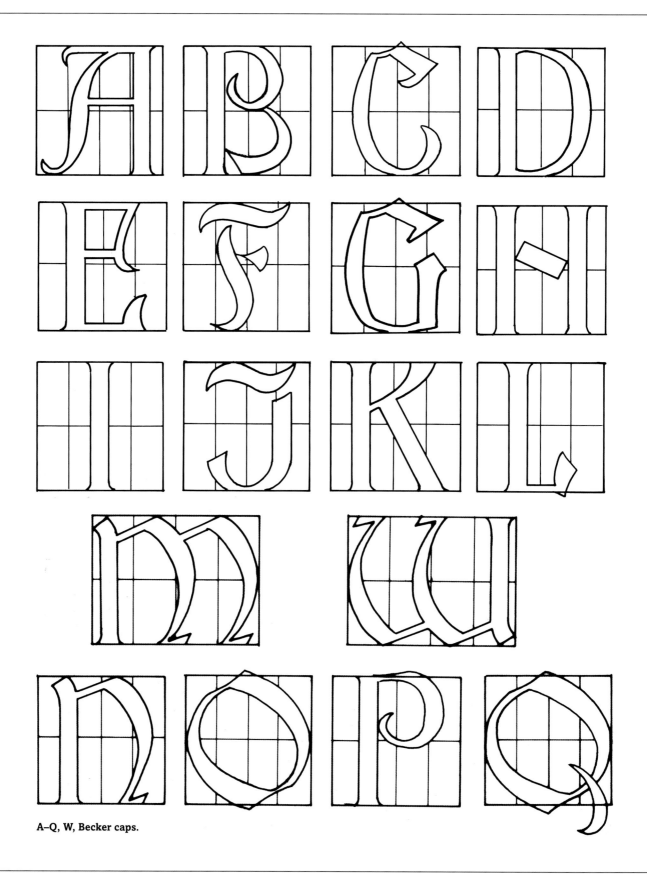

A–Q, W, Becker caps.

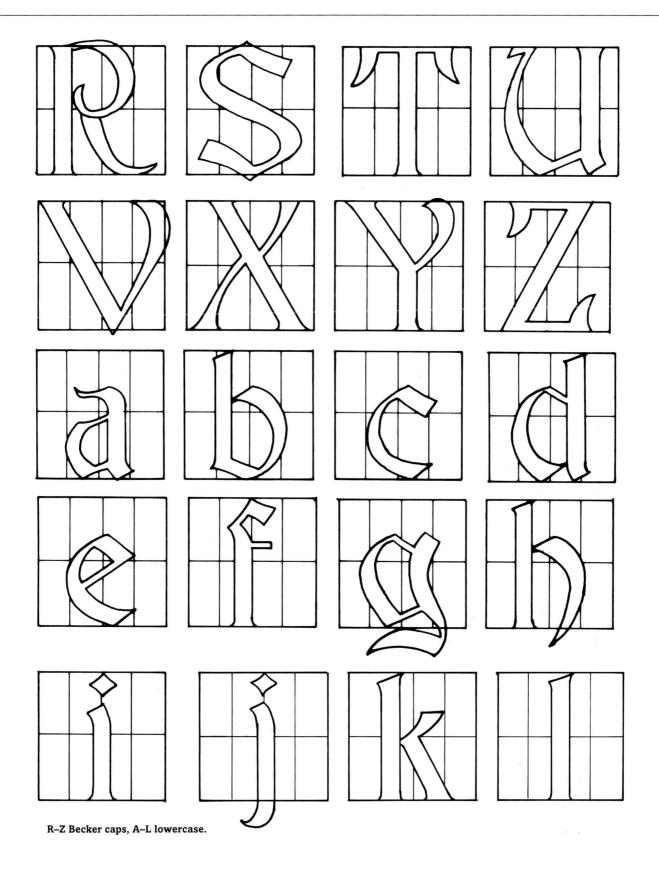

R–Z Becker caps, A–L lowercase.

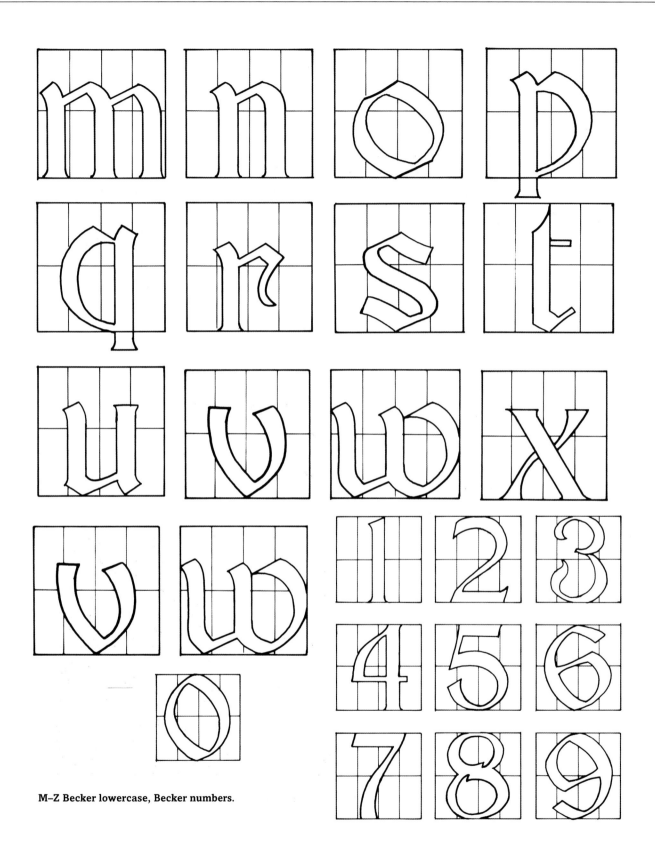

M–Z Becker lowercase, Becker numbers.

Ambrosia

Ambrosia is a condensed typeface that has only capital letters but good anatomy. With its narrow vertical strokes or legs, this style of lettering may be carved larger more easily than those with wider vertical strokes. Also, its condensed nature allows names and words to fit where others cannot.

Ambrosia numbers.

ABCDEF

GHIJKLM

NOPQRS

TUVWX

YZ

Three styles of monogram MB: (top to bottom) Spencerian Script, Neoteric, Barton Capital.

Box panel 12" x 5", basswood classic Roman lettering and numbers.

Box lid 14" x 8½", butternut with script lettering and positive image motif.

Marlies in script.

Foliated letter B.

Foliated letter H.

Barton Capital B.

Napkin holder, basswood with Barton Capital letter B.

Slant lid box 5¹/₂" x 4", basswood with Becker lettering.

8" plate,
basswood with
scalloped border
and Ambrosia
lettering.

Plaque 12" x 9", basswood with free-form motif and altered Becker lettering.

Carvus Maximus.

Plaque 22" x 11¹/₂", butternut stained, with high Gothic lettering MACHS NA (imitate this) from the original stone carving on the cathedral of St. Peter and St. Paul in Bern, Switzerland, 1421 C.E.

FINISHING

13

BECAUSE CHIP-CARVED PIECES often are functional and may be handled frequently, it is recommended that a finish be applied to prevent fingerprints and dirt accumulating over a period of time. Finishing will provide a protected surface that can be dusted and cleaned without harming the wood. Finishing will also enhance the beauty of both the wood and the carving. There are many products and methods available today that may be used for finishing. While the ones described here will serve well, the list is certainly not definitive.

Softer woods such as basswood and butternut respond differently to finishing materials than do harder woods such as walnut and oak. Preparing the wood before any finishing is applied is essential. Remove all pencil marks and lines. This can be facilitated if, when carving, the pencil lines are cut away. Of course, some will always remain and these are easily removed with an ink eraser. If no sharp ridges are present in the carved area, sanding with 220-grit paper may also be helpful. Note that while sanding with a finer grit than 220 will make the wood surface extra smooth, it will also polish it. A highly polished surface may not receive finishing products as well as it would from a surface sanded with 220-grit paper. Always sand with the grain of the wood, never across it.

Methods for Finishing

Woods may be finished by spraying or brushing, but spraying usually gives a more even finish and reduces the possibility of the finish puddling and running in the carved areas. For a natural wood appearance, spray evenly at least three thin coats of satin finish polyurethane. Avoid using glossy finishes, as they subtract from the natural warm appearance of wood. Sand lightly and dust the surface between coats with 220-grit paper, leaving the final coat un-sanded. Whenever spraying or working with finishing products, be sure the work area is very well ventilated and exhausted.

Considerations When Staining

If a carving is going to be stained, it is highly recommended that the procedure first be tested on a similar piece of wood to avoid any unfavorable surprises. Butternut has a strong grain appearance and takes stain very well. Basswood may also be stained, but because it has a tendency to appear mottled when stain is applied, care must be given to the process. Whether using basswood or butternut, spray on a thin coat of polyurethane as a sealer, giving an additional amount to the end grain. This will assist in an even absorption of the stain. Also, after the sealer coat has dried, any grain that is raised by the sealer coat can be sanded with 220-grit to smooth the wood surface before staining.

As mentioned earlier, there are many products available for finishing. However, because gel stains do not penetrate the wood surface or bleed into end grain as much as liquid stains do, and they are chemically compatible with polyurethane, gel stains make a good choice for staining softer woods like basswood and butternut.

With a stiff-bristle artist's brush, work the gel stain into the carved area and over the rest of the wood surface. Wipe off and brush out the excess immediately and let dry. This procedure may have to be repeated to remove all the excess gel stain. If there are spots missed with the gel stain in the carved areas, wait until the stain is dry before going back to cover any missed spots. If the stain already applied is not thoroughly dry, stain fresh from the can will act like a thinner and remove it.

After the stain is thoroughly dry, spray the carving evenly with two or three additional thin coats of satin polyurethane. If sanding between coats is necessary, be careful to do it lightly so as not to sand through the stain.

METRIC EQUIVALENTS

INCHES	MM	CM	INCHES	MM	CM	INCHES	MM	CM
⅛	3	0.3	9	229	22.9	30	762	76.2
¼	6	0.6	10	254	25.4	31	787	78.7
⅜	10	1.0	11	279	27.9	32	813	81.3
½	13	1.3	12	305	30.5	33	838	83.8
⅝	16	1.6	13	330	33.0	34	864	86.4
¾	19	1.9	14	356	35.6	35	889	88.9
⅞	22	2.2	15	381	38.1	36	914	91.4
1	25	2.5	16	406	40.6	37	940	94.0
1¼	32	3.2	17	432	43.2	38	965	96.5
1½	38	3.8	18	457	45.7	39	991	99.1
1¾	44	4.4	19	483	48.3	40	1016	101.6
2	51	5.1	20	508	50.8	41	1041	104.1
2½	64	6.4	21	533	53.3	42	1067	106.7
3	76	7.6	22	559	55.9	43	1092	109.2
3½	89	8.9	23	584	58.4	44	1118	111.8
4	102	10.2	24	610	61.0	45	1143	114.3
4½	114	11.4	25	635	63.5	46	1168	116.8
5	127	12.7	26	660	66.0	47	1194	119.4
6	152	15.2	27	686	68.6	48	1219	121.9
7	178	17.8	28	711	71.1	49	1245	124.5
8	203	20.3	29	737	73.7	50	1270	127.0

[to the nearest mm, 0.1cm, or 0.01m]

CONVERSION FACTORS

1 mm = 0.039 inch
1 m = 3.28 feet
1 m^2 = 10.8 square feet

1 inch = 25.4 mm
1 foot = 304.8 mm
1 square foot = 0.09 m^2

mm = millimeter
cm = centimeter
m = meter
m^2 = square meter

INDEX

ABOUT THE AUTHOR

WAYNE BARTON is a professional woodcarver living in Park Ridge, Illinois, with his wife Marlies—their four children having left the nest. His interest in woodcarving was first kindled at the age of five by his Norwegian grandfather, leaving him with a lifelong love for woodcarving.

Mr. Barton took his formal training in the woodcarving center of Brienz, Switzerland, and his carvings can be found in private collections in Europe, Asia, and North America. He is the only American to have his chip carvings in special exhibition at the Swiss National Museum in Zurich, Switzerland. For the past twenty-two years he has been a columnist for *Chip Chats*, magazine of the National Wood Carvers Association, *Fine Woodworking, American Woodworker, Woodcarving Illustrated,* and other magazines. He has written five other popular books on woodcarving and has made a number of television appearances on *The American Woodshop with Scott Phillips* and *The Woodwright's Shop with Roy Underhill*.

Mr. Barton is the founder and Director of the Alpine School of Woodcarving, Ltd., devoting much of his time to teaching throughout the United States, Canada, and Switzerland. He also has designed and now manufactures chip-carving knives and sharpening stones recognized for their exceptional quality by enthusiasts.

Although versed in all disciplines of carving, he specializes in chip carving and has won both national and international recognition for his work and contributions to the woodcarving community in general.

Wayne Bartons's Web site is: www.chipcarving.com